I0141166

Cover Art and Illustrations: Maria Valentin-Welch

Library of Congress Cataloging-in-Publication Data
Name: Valentin-Welch, Harold, Ray, author
Title: Lamp On a Stand Life Illuminations

Identifiers: ISBN 979-8-9926628-0-1 (pbk.)

LAMP ON A STAND
Life Illuminations

Poems

by

Harold R. Valentin-Welch

No one lights a lamp and then puts it
under a basket. Instead, a lamp is placed
on a stand, where it gives light to everyone
in the house.

Mathew 5:15
NLT

Acknowledgements

I thank my Lord and Savior Jesus Christ for the wonderful gift of salvation. Specifically I thank Him for sending me a guiding angel from Barbados, my grandmother known as Aunt Win, who dragged me to church and introduced me to Christianity. I also thank the Lord for guiding my spirit, focusing my vision, and moving my pencil gripping hand. I've always found solace in writing and have spent many 3 a.m. mornings, when the world is silent, jotting down my conjuring mind.

This work is attributed to my beautiful wife Maria, who always gives her love to the fullest, her encouragement to the highest, and supports all who know her to the upmost. I love you dearly and thank God for the blessing you are in my life.

To my parents Roberta and Sonny, and Harold Sr (RIP), thank you for your examples and positive vibes. Actions truly speak louder than words and your actions on how to live, how to be successful, and how to move forward regardless of circumstances, has always inspired me. I'm fortunate to have your uplifting examples and your love.

To Jay, Chanelle, Kyra, Mariah and Santana, I see your beauty and am proud of all your accomplishments, hard work, endurance and strong spirits. I love you and pray God keeps directing you as you keep finding your way. Tomorrow is the first day of the rest of your lives, make it a good day! Love always.

To the rest of my family and friends, thank you for the supportive relationships, the laughter, the tears and the hope and faith of better days. Also a special acknowledgement goes out to those who helped review this work, my sincere appreciation to you all.

To Massachusetts, the Writers of Color Workshop in Central Square, Cambridge Library (I cherish those times), and the many English teachers from Maynard Grammar School in Cambridge, Cambridge Rindge and Latin High and Northeastern University, I thank you all for your encouragement and professional insight that made you inspire me to keep writing.

These poems are my life illuminations, things observed, felt, experienced and digested. I hope they engage, inspire and awaken every reader into sharing their illuminations too. To God be the glory, be well, be blessed!

Much love and success.
Sincerely,
Harold

Foreword

Heavenly light shone upon me the day I met my wonderful husband, Harold Valentin-Welch, 37 years ago. At the time, I never could have imagined the depth of written inspiration and the God-given gift of words that lived within his soul. Yet, throughout the years, I have had the privilege of hearing his powerful poetry in private readings (I'm your biggest fan, baby!).

We all have reasons to admire our loved ones, but I say this with absolute sincerity— Harold's writing is extraordinary. In an age where AI and software can generate poetry in an instant, my husband remains devoted to his pen and pad, especially in the quiet hours of dawn when the world sleeps and his muse awakens. His words have a way of leaving me in awe—baffled, mesmerized, and deeply moved all at once.

This book has been long in the making. Now that we're embracing our silver-haired years, I know the time has come for him to share this incredible gift with the world. I am beyond proud to introduce his first published masterpiece, *Lamp on a Stand: Life Illuminations*.

This collection takes readers on a journey through Harold's eyes, illuminating five distinct sections of his life:

- **Spotlight** – addressing societal issues that shape our world.

- **Personal Light** – offering glimpses into his life journey and the people who have molded him into the man he is today.

- **Heavenly Light** – reflecting on our faith, our guiding values, and the way we strive to be beacons of God's love in our daily lives.

- **Love Light** – a heartfelt exploration of the power, joy, and heartbreak that love brings. (I secretly hoped this section would be all about me—but love, in its many forms, is a story for all of us.)

- **Sunlight** – a vibrant collection of poetry that touches on various themes, closing with a reminder of poetry's lasting impact on the soul.

We invite you to embark on this journey with us, to let these poems carry you away—if only for a moment—from life's worries and distractions. Walk with us down this poetic memory lane. May these words help you reflect on your own experiences, dreams, and hopes. May they inspire healing, connection, and the realization that we share far more in common than what separates us.

Poetry has a way of speaking directly to the heart. May this book speak to yours.
With love and admiration,
Dr. Maria Valentin-Welch
February, 01, 2025

Contents

Spotlight

The World Aches

The sun rises with a painful glance,
squinting at earth's circumstance.
The blue spherical eye is blackened and sore
from the brutal constant hits of war.

A bomb's pomposity is sharp and cold.
Frozen trees poke the planet with icicles
attempting to cure with acupuncture,
the painful constant hits of war.

The sky drops a snowy white balm
to suppress all weapons with cool calm.
The effort seems to be abhorred
by those executing constant hits of war.

In silent night the great sphere moans,
from ocean fathoms to the cracked ozone.
An ache throbs within earth's core
because of the constant hits of war.

The groaning makes the moon eye squint,
regardless bloodshed won't relent.
The moon hides a half, a quarter, or more,
shamed by the vicious hits of war.

Nature endures with a tearful downpour,
as storms lay siege and tornados breed,
as lightning flashes and thunder clashes,
as fires rage and mudslides cascade.

The atmosphere screams for mercy aloud.
It fears the approaching devastation
from the impending mushroom cloud.

Blue Doorway

Graffiti voices spread across a faded blue door.
Its threshold, an abode where someone has slept
before. Their brown bag of comfort lays empty in this
space. A pillow formed gray sweatshirt remains as a
trace.

Some detest the heads that rest here from day to day.
Perhaps a methodical status-quo system caused this
decay. This vision on a downtown street exposes the
homeless plight. Only this blue doorway knows a
person is missing tonight.

There's a sustained sadness in this memorial shrine,
where residents scrawled epitaphs during their
staying time. This deserted place was left for an
eternal place of rest, its graffiti weeps in memory of
humans discarded as less.

Engraved here are names of not just anyone.
This wooden door displays etched scars
of someone's daughter, someone's son.

Hot Components

(Teenagers are among the highest HIV infected group
in the country *)

Our gadgets surged with power
when our high-speed connectors met
to transmit Twitter desires
hidden in our fiery breaths.

We opened up our laptops
to Facebook in real time.
Erotic jitters subsided
as we touched, caressed, and climbed.

We typed sensual words
on our physical keyboards.
Static gave way to grounded ecstasy
as we tapped away our gems of virginity.

My software turned to hardware
filling your capacity. Blu-ray
sensual encrypted data
burned in our mind's DVD.

We copied programs of love
and pasted bits of intimacy,
as our scrolling fingertips sailed
across our networked bodies.

We painted all the Jpeg pictures
programmed in our minds;
multi-positions mixed with
steady clicks of bumps and grinds.

Our desktops were wallpapered
with icons of graphic love.
The cloud servers hosting our intimacy
preserved our emotions floating above.

We ate Apples and Zoomed visions
of our future teamed positions.
Our day Jobs opened Gates, but
nightly we'd escape to Microsoft embrace.

In TikTok streams we'd share imaginings
of sensual pants and snuggles.
We'd screen-save our red-hot haven
until scans interrupted our signals.

Suddenly our Snapchat pixels
began to lose their hue.
You never told me or never knew
there was a virus inside of you.

Our colorful vector images
of a world with hopeful dreams,
turned to monochrome projections
of flat lines on flat screens.

I wanted to C+ +
as a computer programmer,
you wrote scripts too
while sipping on cups of Java.

A stealthy virus cracked
our security code of love.
Our firewall was breached
and we no longer hug.

An Email of "Promiscuity"
spammed this catastrophe.
Our CPUs now troubleshoot
the root of death's anxiety.

Spontaneity hacked the abstinence
in our anti-virus tools.
Condom security can't reboot
the wireless mode of constant blue.

Our lives have become
raster images of disaster.
The Trojan horse of HIV
threatens to trample faster and faster.

Your modem screams for bandwidth,
my dial-up screams for a lifeline too.
We're relying on a World Wide Web
of pharmaceuticals to see us through.

Refurbish Lord our motherboards
so that we can be, teenagers
falling in love again,
running life's internet virus free.

*CDC statistical data

Mic Consciousness

When I turn on my radio
and hear all the negativity playing;
all I can say is OK, here we go again
another hardcore hand putting a pad to a pen
or should I say a pen to a pad.
It doesn't really matter it's all pretty sad.

When what we need on the mic is positivity
you're just filling up our ears with stupidity.
Injection causing nothing but infection,
your senseless words in our youth show reflection.

Decaying with everything that your saying,
out your mouth in their ear, now they're displaying.
Guns, drugs, gangs, thugs, don't sample,
because this sets a six foot under example.

Stop degrading women with the rough stuff,
of the misogyny I had enough, enough, enough.
So, I stand with mic in hand telling you,
be aware of what the industry is selling you.

Stacks of tracks on wax kicking street facts,
raising and praising the same things that are killing
Latinos, Asians, Caucasians and Blacks,
and society as a whole because we're all entangled.
You lynch one culture we're all strangled.

Now how's that sound, profound? Round and round
we go, plenty of brothers on death row, and with the
metaphors you're steadily readily saying
some have done and with their lives they're paying.

Now I'm wondering what you are
just like that little star. In rap how did you get so far,
with your gangbang kill a man thing
that's devouring and destroying the minds of our
offspring? Sadness and heartaches all you bring.

Mixing up the youth like twister;
Dissing a brother.
          Beating a sister.
Shooting another.
          Killing a mister.
A crying mother.
          A preaching minister,
more hurt by your words that are sinister.

In rap the negativity should be shed,
cause to many of us have already bled.
Young ones run just for fun,
do what you sung; another future's hung.

Now whose throwing lassoes over trees,
cutting off at the knees, stinging like killer bees.
You have Da Youngsters, acting Illegal,
Another Bad Creation that's Kriss Krossed and Lethal.

People, there's something wrong with this,
what we need indeed to lead
the new breed to succeed
is MIC CONSCIOUSNESS!

Scattered Aim

Keep your head on a swivel
and ears pierced for a whistle
of bullets whizzing by
from a firing pistol.
Families are breaking
there's no mistaking
the heartbreak created
from an index finger
intersecting with a trigger.
The bereavement chasm is wide
from murder and suicide,
painful tears drench earth
with hurt a trillion times.
Manufacturers of death
keep widening the breadth,
every bullet in the chamber
represents a life's death.
The NRA crosshairs are on
profitable projections.
Boardroom meetings
keep commercializing the
sales of powerful weapons.
Feigns of presidential green
stream bloodshed repercussion.
A contradiction exists
in their sales pitch
of safety and protection.
The result is fracture
after fracture,
coffin after coffin,
life after life,
after life, afterlife.

Man Unkind

This is man unkind,
a transformed metastasized version of mankind.
A mind, body and soul, kneaded and rolled, until the
taste of humanity turns into an acidic battery,
without the power of love.

This is man unkind,
running into buildings of education
to prematurely book angels for flights to heaven.

This is man unkind,
promising care and autonomy, but delivering
street corner cups of homeless poverty.

This is man unkind,
turning fathers and mothers, sons and daughters,
sisters and brothers, into ballistic missile fodder.

This is man unkind,
living in panic rooms, where lenses zoom-in close
to avoid exchanges of courteous diplomacy.

This is man unkind,
segmented into gated communities of all-inclusive
bliss with community watch activist
killing Skittle carrying kids.

This is man unkind,
where an arm raised, swearing to protect and serve
bends and turns, into a lifeless 6-to-9-minute
chokehold on a fellow citizen.

This is man unkind,
where the political conveyor belt of nepotism keeps
tightening around a taxpayers neck, as we pay
the elite to be kept in their ceiling of debt.

This is man unkind,
where every house has a backyard with a target
backed by a berm, to practice and learn civility.

This is the unkind land of man.

If Education Was a Drug

If education was a drug and we were addicted to the
high, we'd see engineers repairing crack pipe houses
where addiction continues to drown lives.

If education was a drug and we were addicted to the
high, hospital waiting rooms would be nullified by
straight white lines of uniformed doctors
and nurses standing by.

If education was a drug and we were addicted to the
high, we'd hash out our differences in creative ways,
we'd TCB (take care of business)
with THC (the heart cares) toward better days.

If education was a drug and we were addicted to the
high, we'd concentrate our acid hit hallucinations on
rectifying all these racial, hateful, global situations.

If education was a drug and we were addicted to the
high, an overdose would amount to being comatose
to stereotypical bigotry about our cultural identities.

If education was a drug and we were addicted to the
high, Narcan would help us love again,
and understand that greed and money is surpassed
by family and friends.

If education was a drug and we were addicted to the
high, we'd realize we share a planet in demise,
we'd be United Nations attempting to rectify.

But education is not a drug
and we're not addicted to that high.

Personal Light

Famine

I eat the bread of my father's discontent,
chewing the grains of his suffering,
digesting the inner sorrow of his abandonment,
which bloats my belly like a hungered child.

I starve for the father he craves
and so on goes the bread line of the fatherless.
The hunger spreads from grandfather to father to son,
each missing and being a vital part.
Each dying for a fruitful relationship.
Each dying before love is harvested.

The famine grows greater with age
as wisdom reveals the frail and vulnerable
undernourishments; for no one
has taught us to be fathers.

Who will teach us?
We must teach ourselves the way.
Who will teach us to be?
We must learn from day to day.
Who will teach us to be fathers?
Our intuition should lead the way.

The small reflection starving for affection
will teach us to nurture the cause.
Look into your child's eyes and
feed the appetite that once was yours.

Retired

For a moment in time,
I have a clear mind,
no agenda to contend with,
no apprehension.
This factory of bones
no longer burns brain cells
to manufacture a pension.

For a moment in time,
my production isn't mass
produced by winding gears
of a timeclock.
Work screens no longer
sift my dreams,
alpha numeric keys
no longer keep me locked.

For a moment in time,
I no longer bebop or hip hop
to bars of corporate events
to pose in company illustrations
of successful sophistication.
My network isn't my net worth,
and I can hear the triumphant
orchestral sound of peace
broadcasting over my anxieties.

For a long time, my life time
laid on an economic alter,
submerged in the acquisition
of someone else's procured vision,
that once seemed so sublime,
until this moment in time.

Mutiny Of Wrinkled Skin

The uprising of wrinkled skin
waves a cross-bone flag of rebellion.

Seditious villains from deep within
emerge wearing an Alzheimer's grin.

Arthritic joints crackle and applaud
as organs moan dirges and sad songs.

Blood seeps through varicose veins
as arteries harden throughout the days.

Diabetes swings its horrid axe
separating limbs as it attacks.

Pirates apprehend the flesh land,
as time spills through clenched hands.

Powerful fists now succumbed
to a bandit's merciless beating drum.

Time ravenously snatches life
its golden hook twinkles in twilight.

Soon all the portals will close,
no breathe will flow through chest or nose.
Homeward bound the spirit goes.

We navigate life's sea for nautical gains,
beginning to end, and then just remains.

But on the journey we can delight
as we plot our legacy of life.

Headstones are marked born and gone,
but in between life's bounty floats on.

Love and friendships are the ships,
that transcend deaths ominous grip.

Storms and hardships come and go,
waves crest high and seas bellow low.

Sail your vessel steady through all the squalls
as the wrinkled skin of mutiny evolves.

Writing Insanity

I cast out a line
let the reel run tangible
let it bob on the waves
of the Papyrus Sea
my exhausted grip loosens
as the lead rod extends
heavy in the grasp
waiting patiently
for punctuation

I move my mind at times,
with graphite pole in hand.
I climb out on slippery rocks,
as my thoughts command.
I dangle from heights
of vulnerability, expecting to catch
the unexpected in a catchphrase.
I'm exposed to misty instability
where emotions can push me off,
and I lose the hook baiting
my initial thought.

I cast out a line
let the reel run tangible
let it bob on the waves
of the Papyrus Sea
my exhausted grip loosens
as the lead rod extends
heavy in the grasp
waiting patiently
for punctuation

I move my mind at times,
with graphite pole in hand...

Dual Flight

Upon exiting my
room of existence,
I turned off the light switch
and there on the other side
of my windowpane,
catching my attention
like a soft caress,
a firefly was working
its intermittent illumination
through variable
moon beam situations.

I watched the dancing
strobe wander deeper,
forging a path through
a world of woods.
I flicked my light switch
on and off several times
in solidarity with the firefly.
Likewise, the radiant captain replied.

The starry darkness emitted
the pixel process of all beings
navigating their plights
through the unknown night.

Beau

Physically it's true that we all must go
and you are physically gone.

With our eyes fixed in the spiritual we
see the joy and laughter lingering on.

Your smile and demeanor always lifted
a weary down cast soul.

My uncle, my brother, my friend,
your memory could never go.

It resides immortal inside all who had
the pleasure of knowing you.

Within each, you deposited a joyful jewel
more valuable than any treasure.

To know you was our pleasure, and now
the only comfort is to know
that Beau knows, peace.

Winifred

My grandmother took me to see
Billy Graham's Library.
She was a praying woman,
known as Aunt Win to a community
of bottle feeders, and diaper wearers.
The pupils are all grown up now
without any recollection of her.
But I was a witness to her
biblical acts of Jesus.

My grandmother took me to see
Billy Graham's Library.
She'd listen to his sermons
broadcasting across her days.
She'd give God praise
with every child she helped raise.
She'd shelter some unfortunate ones
when relatives weren't acting relevant.

My grandmother took me to see
Billy Graham's Library. I entered
through the foot of the glass cross
holding my wife's hand, holding
emotions in. Billy Graham's voice
made me wish I could hear Aunt Win's
once again, singing names, lifting spirits.
Her daily actions preached a loving
sermon without a podium.

I looked toward the Charlotte, NC sky
tracing grandma's silhouette with clouded eyes.
My pupils were raining with her loving memories,
that took me to see Billy Graham's Library.

American Beauty??

With a *Cry Freedom* voice I exclaimed,
"What! Denzel Washington didn't win!"
Some *Devil in a Blue Dress* must of
caused this Academy Award dysfunction.

It's a *Carbon Copy* of a black *Soldier's Story*,
our butts can go to war,
our bodies can go to the *Bone Collector*,
but still, we get no *Glory*.

A *Hurricane* win was denied once again.
History repeats itself because like Mr. Carter,
Denzel the *Mighty Quinn*, also deserves
his hand raised high as champion.

He Got Game, Denzel shines
like the *Philadelphia* star Doctor J.
His class, style and acting repertoire
highlights his talents and *Virtuosity*.

In the past the *Scent of a Women*
caused Denzel Oscar winning strife.
This time I thought a change would occur
because of prayers from *The Preacher's Wife*.

But Oscar 2000 was a *Ricochet* back to Oscar 1993,
when the captivating *Power* of *Malcolm X*
was masterly portrayed on screen
by Denzel Washington and director Spike Lee.

Both award ceremonies smelled like a *Mississippi
Masala* soaked in a swamp stench of *Crimson Tide*.
Both years the Academy Award members took
a true black man's story for a flirtatious virgin ride.

Maybe Oscar 2000 had *Mo' Better Blues*.
The Oscar gang was missing. Oddly the golden boys
and ballots had *Fallen* under *The Siege* of unknown
hands, but soon returned polished
 and glistened with decision.

The prominent statues probably peeked at
the ballots and hid because of shame and disbelief.
They might as well of had *Courage Under Fire*
in the rear end of a *Pelican Brief* exercising relief.

I served *For Queen and Country* that night,
my wife Maria and I watched for 4 hours long.
The Spacey outcome nearly caused a *Heart Condition*,
because the choice for best actor was
surprisingly wrong.

Academy how can your aptitudes of judging say
that Denzel Washington didn't win?
I could have watched *St. Elsewhere*,
because Oscar 2000 you were "*Much Ado About
Nothing*!"

Heavenly Light

Everlasting Fireworks

A sparkle, a burst, a bright light,
over thousands of faces colors ignite;
the beauty of it all can't compare
to the moon and the stars God places in the air.
Firework colors abound, symphonies sound,
but when daybreak arises it is over.

Sunrays flare bright to wave goodbye to the night.
Cotton clouds march forth bringing the daylight.
A wonderful parade flows across the sky
revealing God's power to the human eye.

On the horizon I see God's majestic glory.
His power does reign, His strength unchanged.
For granted we take the fireworks He makes,
the music He plays, God daily displays.
Oh why, oh why don't we gather to see
the everlasting fireworks of God the Almighty?

Firework celebrations simply can't compare
to God's beauty that is everlasting and everywhere.
True freedom, independence and love
only God can give. He sent his son Jesus
to carry our cross, and everyday God proves He lives!

Oceans

God gives water its free will
and it will flow as it will.

He's watched a sea of people boating
to escape tragedy.

He's seen chaotic squalls of humans
raging for food to eat.

He's watched the flow of walking water
flooding borders for liberty.

He's seen hordes of misled white caps
pounding against democracy.

He's watched the trickling of metal barrels
create holes in flesh and marrow.

He's seen the dammed water clogged
by vials, needles and coke straws.

He's watched the swift water of suicide
wreck family shorelines when it collides.

He's seen economic undertow collapse
bridges, keeping shelter at a distance.

He's watched brackish water slamming
on piers of bones built by famine.

He's seen scenes of deep dark waves
rise up from being slaves.

He's watched the cleansing of tsunamis
when quakes of hate raise up armies.

He's seen beaches of chunky chum
from warring drunkards of red rum.

He's scanning humanity's horizon
for a peaceful continent or island.

One day the drowning tides will subside
and God will be glorified.

J3OHN16 Vaccine

I feel the
world's
sharpness
grinding
against
my soul,
Holy hands keep uplifting my heart. I
hang out selfishly, reluctant to believe
the pulsating fact that I'm a child of God.
Then I feel the
nails piercing
deep into flesh,
the sacrificing of
a heart on a hill,
the hanging of
bones on a cross,
desiring to forgive
a world, desiring
to forgive a soul,
desiring to forgive
me. The pulsating
act of love keeps
infusing belief,
revealing that I
am resurrected
from the tombs
of this world. I
am a child of God.

Keep Your Hand

Strive, survive, spiritually stay alive.
We have the victory, it's proved in history
when God is on your side.
Greater is He that is in me
than he that is trying to bring a frown.
I know my God won't let me down.
So, in the middle of heartbreak and danger,
I call on God, cause He's the master rearranger.
For your life He has a prosperous plan, understand.
So, keep your hand in the hand of the one who can.

Repent from sin, open up your heart.
Allow God to give you a new start.
He can do it right away, today,
ask Him to come into your life and He'll stay.
If you don't understand, let me explain;
God came into my life and made a change.
He took away the sorrow and pain,
replaced it with sunshine,
but even in the pouring rain
on the Solid Rock I stand because
I keep my hand in the hand of the one who can.

Pour out your soul, let God take control.
The broken pieces of your life God can mold.
He can make you, shape you, rearrange you,
just give it to God, cause God can do!
Anything that you need He'll provide.
He put the Holy Spirit inside to guide.
We have the power any hour to bloom,
through any raging sea situation God can part room.
He'll take you to your Canaan Land, understand,
So, keep your hand in the hand of the one who can.

Relax, exhale, take a breath.
Give your life to God before nothings left.
Worldly ways keep you in a daze.

God can remove the smoke and the haze.
Clouded by all life's pressure,
allow God to work and He'll bless ya.
When temptation to do wrong comes along,
resist remember the words of this poem.
You can overcome, yes you can, if you just,
keep your hand in the hand of the one who can.

For Better; Leave It For Ever

For a better life,
put down the pipe.
Pick up biblical words of life.
Let them encompass your brain.
We need a compass to plot
our course, we need the power
of God's spiritual force.

For a better life,
put down the alcohol.
No need to be commercialized,
at all, by the one-eyed screen.
Tell-lie-vision shows the highs,
not the lows, or the toe tags
bound on a cirrhosis liver's toes.

For a better life,
put down the drugs.
No need to rely on a product
to addict us to false love.
True love comes from
God above.
We can't replace him
with artificial infatuation.

Playground

My spirit lives within
a perimeter of fenced skin,
organs are my swings,
bones my jungle gym.

At times I merry-go-round.
I monkey bar on a rib cage,
I climb up an artery
and slide down a vein.

When it's time to depart
this sandbox life on loan,
God will shake the granules
from my earthly clothes.

This life's skinned knees, scars,
aches, pains, mental wounds,
scrapes and fractured bones,
will all be healed when
I reach my heavenly home.

Until then I'll employ myself
in God's great creation.
Once exhausted I'll rest well,
in the comfy home of heaven.

Granny Smith, Aunt Win, Mr. and Mrs. Ricketts

There's an old leather bible with
pages painted with colored pencils.
It belonged to a lady I would often see;
with closed eyes, praying hands, and bended knees.
The lady always prayed for you and me.
She'd reach out to the Lord in prayer,
because the Trinity is always there.
Even though the lady may be gone,
her prayers are a lasting legacy
that remains to keep us strong.

If you have a praying person in your life,
providing you with God's guiding light,
it's a blessing. It's a blessing!

There's a closed door with silence,
with a man praying behind it.
Amongst the city noise and violence,
he searches bible scriptures for God's divine guidance.
The man always prayed for you and me.
He'd reach out to the Lord in prayer,
because the Trinity is always there.
Even though the man may be gone,
his prayers are a lasting legacy
that remains to keep us strong.

If you have a praying person in your life,
providing you with God's guiding light,
it's a blessing. It's a blessing!

Prayer brings God's favor,
gives us the protection of the Savior,
steers us in the right direction,
when we have bad behavior.
That's why we're successful,
beat the haters and the rivals.

Prayer is the very essence
of our daily survival.
It explains why we have plenty,
It's not because we're lucky.
People always prayed for you and me.
Praying is important for us to be.

So let's pray for one another,
ask God's blessing for each other.
Fill the desolate atmosphere,
with hope, faith and loving prayer.

Graduate

We live within this spherical classroom
surrounded by a ceiling of clouds and stars.
Lessons are daily taught to us
that are uniquely ours.

There are tests that test our heart's sum
and hard problems arise in the curriculum,
but there's a Teacher who's cap and gown
is a heavenly robe and golden crown.

Life will have its twist and turns
and throughout we continue to learn.
God gave us a great course book to follow.
This textbook of life is called the bible.

Who

Who put the green in the trees and the blue in the sky,
who blessed your eye to see it all, when your favorite
players playing ball?

Who created the world gave it a twirl and it still
rotates, who's masterful with everything
that He creates?

Who parted the Red Sea, created you and me,
made the blind see and keeps us continually?

Who makes the waves roll, makes the winds blow,
makes the world sunny, shower, rain and snow?

Who has the wisdom to design the solar system
and create in every human eleven life systems?

Who pours down water from heaven,
divides salty from fresh, so all things keep living?

Who gave many nations various pigmentations,
and uses a colorful palette in forming His creations?

Who defines a timeline, makes planets align
and allows sunshine when the moon declines?

Who flashes lightning with thunderous sound,
that reaches the world and strikes the ground?

Who architects small designs in a microscope
and murals large landscapes in a telescope?

Who developed the earth's crust, sprinkled islands
like dust, and hung the sun in the sky
to warm all of us?

Who paid the ultimate cost, sent His Son to the cross
to express His Love for us, so we wouldn't be lost?

Who? The Lord God Almighty!
Who? The Lord God Almighty!

If you don't know, now you know,
that the Lord God Almighty is in control!

Love Light

She Dug Me

She looked
deep in the dirt
I was buried in
and saw enriching
soil in my soul.
She dug me,
sweetly,
with her laugh,
gently with her eyes,
softly with her touch.

Her ways of restoration
converted my condemnation.
Love and I were obliged
to walk on opposite sides, past
encounters dispensed my feelings.
My eyes were drenched in futile rain.
My heart was buried in a casketed frame.

Nevertheless, she looked deep, she dug me,
and in that digging
a seed was planted.
Now our flower
of love is the tallest,
most beautiful one,
in a world full
of wild weeds.

Origami

I fold myself into you.
Each crease celebrates our union.
We were once flat and unattached to love
but now our paper hearts
align with purpose.

You fold yourself into me.
Love takes shape around
sharp corners of this world.
We hold each other in personal places,
curve together through tragic spaces.
We bend into a tender form
all our own.

In the dark angles of life,
our love forms mutual support
and our edges of cherished moments
expand to cover the rips and tears
of solemn days.

An artwork emerges from our intimacy.
Papyrus hearts transform into
three-dimensional beauty,
displaying the volume of love
created in each turn
of you and me.

When life tries to twists under
our love infinitely folds
over and over to cover
the pain again and again.

Birds of Indecision

We lay like shucked shells
on a sea salt beach, sweaty
waves cascade over our continents.
A breezy satisfaction carries
a lovebird's melody.
Through my open mind
birds are sweetly singing across the sea.

I envision the unity of us
laying in togetherness,
but we choose to be
inanimate voids of incompleteness.

My dissolute ways are converting
to sing affectionate hymns,
but we choose to be
abandoned by commitment.

Our extreme attraction plays
concertos of fleshly passion,
but we choose to be
a pretense of symphonic fidelity.

Love is persuading me
to write a treaty that would open up
the borders of our hearts.

"Marry me," would be the phrase
that would begin a beautiful deep
journey into each other's territory.

I love you, but from afar
shrilling seagulls cry out,
"Naaahhh, Naaahhh,"
what obnoxious scavengers they are.

Sonnet of Hidden Tears

When the heart is swooned it cries blood tears.
The arteries continually pulsate to beat.
No drops to see will form among the years,
inside resides the pain of hearts defeat.

The years attempt to show the strain of all,
because we're wrapped in skin that moves in time.
But no one can see the depth of the skin shawl,
its wrinkled art of pain does weave a rhyme.

To all that hold a lost love that cannot be;
rest assure the aching vestment that's worn,
is a cloak that many cannot begin to see,
few will know your heart has been so torn.

Sweet love will always throb inside your shell,
where the enduring ache of loss will always dwell.

Lacuna

It is like a missing molar;
the mechanics of chew remain,
the up and down, open and close,
the grinding of daily matter
is similar but not the same.

Each bite of day
smiles a yellow stain.

Each swallow of night
decays the ivory moon.

That is how I count my steps
on the pedometer of years.

Long strides slither
over a jagged canyon
your departure created,
when you were ripped away
from the ground of my world.

Love's Reflection

The curve of your spine and mine align.
Parallel is the love we share.
No longer do we dangle
in selfish atmospheres.
We have become one,
beating in sync.
Feel our hearts,
we do
love.
Love,
we do.
Feel our hearts
beating in sync.
We have become one.
In selfish atmospheres
no longer do we dangle.
Parallel is the love we share.
The curve of your spine and mine align.

Flowers

Today I give you flowers of all kinds
so the colorful bouquet of my love
is a lingering scent in your mind.

May Dandelions roar
in the jungle of our love,
and Marigolds reflect the
valuable treasures in our hugs.

When angered may Poppy's pop
to make our Bleeding Hearts heal,
as we cuddle sipping honey love
from a brew of Chamomile.

May African Violets run wild
and free without being provoked,
as Birds of Paradise circle above
cawing, "you are the most."

May Crocuses jump and croak
with the deep affection that we feel,
as Morning Glories awaken
our daily dose of splendid appeal.

May we ride on petals of Camellias
through seasons of winter blight,
and hope hedges of Laurels
protect us from argumental frost bite.

In adorned cribs Babies Breaths will
giggle and smile at our love's success,
as Evergreens burst berry dreams
that cradle us in happiness.

In sprawling fields Daisies lean
to hail you as my beautiful queen,
as the eyes of Irises open wide
as you walk by in royal stride.

Orchids debate and orchestrate
the grand colors our hearts create.
Red Roses invert their prickly thorns
to play you a tribute on their green horns.

The Daffodils can't sit still
they dance to the wonderful tune,
as Lilacs extend their throats
to serenade you in the silvery moon.

Lilies dress all nice and frilly
because the party has begun.
All the flowers pay homage
to you my love, because
you're the most beautiful one.

Sunlight

Can-It-Be-Us

Can it be us; the finest home grown
picked to be stoned pillars of success,
flourishing stems with branches that
never end, budding exotic blends
into the bloodstream of mainstream?

Can it be us; sticks of contention,
seeds of disrespecting, all crumbled,
cleaned and sifted, so we can be lifted
to a natural nature of humane stature?

Can it be us; rolled into a condensed concentration
of conception, lit by the belief that God can
empower our souls and rejuvenate our minds
into well-being regardless of how much
presidential paper we're rolled in?

Can it be us; deeply inhaling all
the smoke and malign wind, holding...
and exhaling cool life positions that
swirl streams of positivity toward heaven?

Can it be us; composting all the waste
into fertilized knowledge, growing
scholarly vines that break ceilings, and climb
with stems, budding cap and gown exhilarations,
instead of seedy incarcerations?

Can it be us; puffing and passing on life's essence,
feeling comfortably high, clipping onto a completion
of a lovely lifelong drag, and burning the living joint
all the way down to the clips very end, before
the ashes descend, and our spirits ascend?

I'm not talking about cannabis smoking.
I'm talking about toking on a well rolled good life.

Recognize Your Gift

Hate is an ill fate. I definitely negate that state.
I'd rather stimulate and demonstrate
the poetic landscape we
break ground on, break bread on,
that fed up heads are fed on.
While takers take, fakers fake,
haters hate, and love breakers
keep breaking up the L-O-V-E,
let me poetically tell you about we.

We Sojourner Truth in the atmosphere.
Poetic sunrays shine lucid light in deaf ears.

We're verbally staking claim flags,
spraying on provocative name tags,

and painting injustices of past history.
We're taking back our rightful territory.

Poetic power is what we use; we fuse
in verbal rivers like Langston Hughes.

Our ink quenches those who are thirsting
we're writing strong like Zora Neale Hurston.

The beat of our song I thought you knew
we groove steadily like Maya Angelou.

There is no height too far above us
we can reach stars like Fredrick Douglas.

Sometimes though the sadness is sudden
and we cry tears of Countee Cullen.

Nevertheless, we keep making a way
moving with our words like Claude McKay.

We verbalize and show abstract love
soaring to poetic heights like Rita Dove.

So, keep the ink synergy flowing,
flex those skillful pens on poems,

and in the midst of any scandal,
Quote the "Analysands" by Dudley Randall.

When there continues to be contempt
keep writing like Arna Bontemps.

Our writing styles are working constantly
Strutting, "Black Power" like Nikki Giovanni.

Our sounds are lifting and bobbing heads,
syncopating rhythms like Sonia Sanchez.

We're fighting daily madness with inspiration,
getting on, moving along with iambic vibrations.

Beating the odds like Paul Robeson,
proud to be one of God's gifted scribe children.

We're writing notes of hope that inspire,
igniting verbal fire like Yusef Komunyakaa.

We're telling the youth they can win,
fighting the social isms like James Baldwin.

Psychologically we're escaping the bars,
freeing minds like Paul Lawrence Dunbar.

Our souls intellectually speak with a voice
reflecting thoughts of W.E.B. Dubois.

No longer are we invisible women and men
our quills show ills like Ralph Ellison.

Our history runs deeper than oceans,
explore and teach facts like June Jordan.

Our indelible ink rises like the sun
write it all down like Toni Morrison.

When bruises of life turn purple on ya
color them over like Alice Walker.

The strength of your heritage will never fail,
be proud like Alex Haley and tell the tale.

In the aftermath of capital storming
Stand firm and recite hope like Amanda Gorman

Through pain, love, conflict and slander,
hold up the banner like Kwame Alexander.

Keep the rhythm and rap words tight,
in the name of Richard Wright, write alright.

Let the pulsating ink flow from the heart,
display true expressions in written art.

Haiku, God bless you!

"Writing So Sweetly"
Our poetic words
are waving in the cool breeze
like Phillis Wheatley

Haiku, God bless you!

"Liquid Poetry"
In Gwendolyn Brooks
poetry floats us upstream.
Swim in her deep words.

Poetic creations are insightful restorations,
built on ancestral grounds that are sound.

WE are a reach one, teach one, writing nation,
under a thunderous poetic vibration.

WE put asunder vile nations and notions
with word depths of intellect, that stir
the mind, heart and soul.

Sometimes half of me is missing
and poetry makes me whole.

So, after a long day I verbally stroll,
mentally walk in my poetic garden.
I skip happily through reminiscences,
I back flip through pages of poetic forefathers.
They spiritually handed down a gift.
Their sweet aroma causes attitudes to shift.
With the power of poetry, Brothers and Sisters...
Continue to uplift...Continue to uplift...
Recognize your gift!

Glimmer

We share the same air,
the same space in time.
Your blood runs red
and so does mine.
Our ancestors misinterpreted
the treasures we'd find,
if we'd only acknowledge
that we're two of a kind.

Hearts pump to rhythms
that are equal.
Our shared life experiences
could write a good sequel.
If we'd only recognize
we're not gods, just people,
encapsulated in tinged bodies
that fade from strong to feeble.

With strength, let's work together
to break the prejudice mold
and discover the values
our cultures do hold.
Our unity could begin to unfold
the God-given richness of life,
the glimmering gold.

Scrimshaw

These bones are marking earth.
There is a carving out
that happens everyday
in the tides of waking and sleeping.
An artistry is created in being a human being.

The daily design surrenders life to time,
as it generates an intricate space
of inherent value all its own.

In the end, remnants
of inspiration or degradation
lay etched in the skeletal artistry
of coffin framed ivory.

There is a message left
in the life carving of bones,
as they engrave their way
through night and day.

Every day in the wake, the ability
to indelibly construct a pattern
of optimism or pessimism exist.

As lifeless figures the bones still
inspire life, or infuse life with death,
for those examining the history
to decipher the legacy left.

Unusual Harvest
Dedicated to the "Strange Fruit" that suffered so...

They were macabre gifts,
those peeled avocados
dangling from southern vines.
The large-hearted seeds endured vile times.

The citrus blood of our lifeline subsisted,
though it was singed, juiced and twisted.
It was a pulpy sacrifice.
Sweet marmalade life
was glazed by racist light.

A setting sun kissed the dried-up rinds.
Tomatoes in dreadful red remnants
were slashed from the life vine.
The fruit was left to meet death.

The cold sebaceous olives
pitted with bulging red eyes,
saw hope bloom as they slipped
into the slipknot of tragic night.

The passion fruit was drenched
in cherubs' silent cries.
They received the anointing
from the saturated skies.

Ditched were the pomegranates.
Planted were multi-seeds of prosperity.
Sweet papaya grew in the perverse
caricature of pale humanity.

The fruit survived over 400 years
of brutal winter tyranny.
Today the harvest grows
in the accomplishments of you and me.

57

Ghetto Window Sorrow, Spirit...Rocket, Dazzle, Fly

Great minds are born and die in the ghetto.
Here I've watched intellect decay in my window.
Each face somehow reflects a lineage of sorrow.
Too many have swallowed the bitters that kill the spirit.
Total disenfranchisement is a ticket on poverty's rocket.
Only determined individuals can create their dazzle.

When backdrops pop with gunshots glaring dazzle
In hallways littered with syringes of the ghetto,
Never believe your heart can't skyrocket.
Don't resign or decline, shine through skeptical windows.
Only trust your ability to overcome the impoverished spirit.
Warped attitudes turn hope into doubtful sorrow.

So, stand on a plan to overcome the forecasted sorrow.
Over time your positive sunshine will begin to dazzle.
Release the chains that anchor your mighty spirit.
Ride a positive consciousness that deflects thinking ghetto.
Oppose the staccato view and create a symphony window
Where optimism charts a positive course for your rocket.

So, fuel your mind with the knowledge to blast your rocket.
Plan to be the future, only you can divert the storm of sorrow.
Inhale hope, carry it in your lungs, and fog the ghetto window.
Reign over your destiny with sunny burst that dazzle.
Invest in who you want to be, you don't have to be ghetto.
Triumph over poverty by utilizing your mind and spirit.

Remember, strength starts with what you feed it. Good spirit
Only enhances the chances of outer limit flights for your rocket.
Carefully set your sights for a fantastic flight out the ghetto.
Kick in prejudice doors that attempt to submerse you in sorrow.
Encompass your heart with the brilliance of your dazzle.
Tomorrow destiny will shine through a panoramic window.

Drench your mind in the sunshine by opening a hopeful window.
Advance to a higher crescendo, release the doves of your spirit.
Zoom to a better state of mind and watch your fireworks dazzle.
Zigzag your angles around the nonsense and fly your rocket
Legitimate and high through the clouded sky of sorrow.
Extrude your vision with precision, get your mind out the ghetto.

Forget the window's view and ignite the flight of your rocket.
Let your heart fly free and your spirit will triumph over sorrow.
Your dazzling determination will alter the vision of the ghetto.

The Poets I Know

The poets I know
are not known.
They are sprawled on
pages yet unborn.
They lay in sheets
not incubators.
They refuse to be
space invaders.
Letter by letter
they walk the land.
By word of mouth
they spread their clan.
To their resort
there's no quick guide.
Their artistic gifts
in heart reside.
No tome or tomb
shows their resilience.
Word by word
they extend their brilliance,
by observing the world,
leaving no unturned stone.
The poets I know
are probably reading this poem.
Some may be intending,
some may be bold,
some yet have tablets,
laptops or pencils to hold.
But if you're reading this
then I know, you might
be one of the poets
I know.
Iron they say sharpens
iron. I hope you're
one poet I'm inspiring.

www.ingramcontent.com/pod-product-compliance
Lightning Source LLC
Chambersburg PA
CBHW052215090426

42741CB00010B/2553